Contents

	Solo Book	Accompaniment Book
BAGATELLE -Hovey & Leonard	8	19
CONCERT PIECE - Hovey & Leonard	4	6
FOLKSONG FOR CLARINET - Schumann/arr. Belden	10	24
LA CZARINE - Ganne/arr. Hovey & Leonard	12	32
LITTLE PIECE - Schumann/ed. Shifrin/arr. Erickson	2	16
PRELUDE - Jarnefelt/arr. Lowry	11	28
SCHERZINO - Andersen/arr. Waln	6	10
STAR FALL - Belden	14	38
VALSE GRAZIOSO - Hovey & Leonard	3	2
WALTZ from COPPELIA - Delibes/arr. Hovey & Leonard	16	46

CLASSIC FESTIVAL SOLOS, Volume 2 is a counterpart to the companion, Volume 1. Idiomatic solo materials with an eye to variety and playability are included, beginning with easier material and progressing to more difficult.

Works from several periods of composition are presented to give the advancing student the opportunity to learn and to demonstrate performance in each appropriate style. Technical progression is taken into consideration as well as program appeal for both soloist and audience.

Jack Lamb, Editor

VALSE GRAZIOSO

NILO W. HOVEY & BELDON LEONARD

Tempo di valse

4

CONCERT PIECE

NILO W. HOVEY & BELDON LEONARD

EL03874

SCHERZINO

JOACHIM ANDERSON, Op. 55, No. 6
Arranged by GEORGE WALN

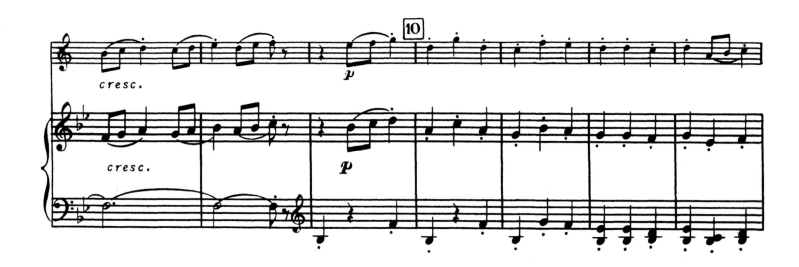

12

LITTLE PIECE

ROBERT SCHUMANN
Edited by DAVID SHIFRIN
Arranged by FRANK ERICKSON

BAGATELLE

NILO W. HOVEY & BELDON LEONARD

EL03874

FOLKSONG FOR CLARINET

ROBERT SCHUMANN
Arranged by GEORGE R. BELDEN

*Note: The quarter note triplet pattern may be changed to ♩ ♫ if it is too advanced.

Piano

PRELUDE

ARMAS JARNEFELT
Arranged by ROBERT LOWRY

LA CZARINE
Mazurka

LOUIS GANNE
Arranged by HOVEY-LEONARD

STAR FALL

GEORGE R. BELDEN

EL03874

WALTZ FROM "COPPELIA"

DELIBES
Arranged by HOVEY-LEONARD